DATE DUE

New 4-22-87

FEB 1 8 1993

MAY 2 1 1987   NOV 2 2 1996          MAY 1 1 2003

JUL 8 1987    DEC 2 8 1996          JUL 2 0 2004

NOV 0 1 1997

SEP 8 1987

DEC 2 1 1988                        AUG 2 5 2009

OCT 2 8 1989   MAR 2 5 1998   AUG 1 0 2011

APR 1 0 1990  APR - 1 1998

SEP 1 3 2011

MAY 2 8 1991   APR 2 9 1998  MAR 3 1 2012

NOV 7 - 1991  JUL 1 7 2003  AUG 2 0 2012

DEC 1 9 1991  MAR 2 9 2006  DEC 2 3 2013

APR 2 0 1992

JUN 2 2 1992

AUG 1 7 1992              APR 0 5 2016

NOV 3 0 1992

*Copyright* © Joanna Troughton 1979, 1986
*Reprinted 1983*
*New Edition 1986*

*First published in 1979 by*
Blackie and Son Limited, Furnival House, 14-18 High Holborn, London WC1V 6BX.

British Library Cataloguing in Publication Data
Troughton, Joanna
How rabbit stole the fire.
I. Title
823'.914[J] PZ7

ISBN 0-216-91834-0

*First American edition published in 1986 by*
Peter Bedrick Books, New York

Library of Congress Cataloging-in-Publication Data
Troughton, Joanna.
   How rabbit stole the fire.

   Summary: Retells the traditional Indian legend of how Rabbit managed to steal
fire from the Sky People and bring it to Earth.
   1. Indians of North America—Legends. [1. Indians of North America—Legends]
   I. Title.
E98.F6T76     1986     398.2'08997     85-15629
ISBN 0-87226-040-2

Printed in Great Britain by Cambus Litho, East Kilbride

Folk-tales of the World

# How Rabbit Stole the Fire

*Joanna Troughton*

**Blackie**
London

**Bedrick/Blackie**
New York

*Author's Note*

This story of rabbit and how he
brought fire to the earth comes from
the South East of the USA and is told
by the Creek, the Hitchiti and the
Koasati Indians. Stories of rabbit the
trickster and wonder worker are
found in all the areas east of the
Mississippi from Hudson Bay to the
Gulf of Mexico.

In the beginning there was no fire
on Earth, and the world was cold.

The Sky People had fire.
But they lived high up in
the mountains, and guarded
it from the animals.

"Who will steal the fire?"
asked the animals, when
the leaves began to fall
and the cold winds blew.

The bison was strong.
The wolf was cunning.
The bear was brave.
The wildcat was fierce.

But Rabbit was leader
of them all in mischief.

Rabbit made himself a wonderful
head-dress. Each feather, every
stitch he coated with pine resin.

"Here I go," said Rabbit, putting
on the wonderful head-dress.
And off he went to the village
of the Sky People. As he went
he sang a song. "Oh, I am going
to fetch the fire, to fetch the
fire, to fetch the fire." For that
is what he was going to do.

"Here is Rabbit,"
muttered the Sky People.
"He is a liar. He is a trickster.
He is the chief mischief-maker.
Do not trust him."

"Hallo, Sky People," said Rabbit.
"I have come to teach you a new dance.
Look at my dancing hat.

It is a dance to bring the corn from
the earth. It is a dance to guide
the fish to your nets."

So spoke Rabbit the trickster.
And with his words he soothed the Sky
People. He charmed them. He flattered them.

They forgot that he was a mischief-maker
and welcomed him into their village.
"Rabbit shall lead us in the dance!"

So Rabbit led the dance!
Round and round the fire
danced Rabbit. And round and
round behind him danced the
Sky People. Round and round
danced Rabbit, wearing his
wonderful head-dress . . .

and as he danced, he bent low
to the fire, singing his
dancing song. And the Sky
People bent low also.
Round and round danced Rabbit,
and very low he bent . . .

Whoosh! The head-dress was alight!
And away raced Rabbit, out of
the village and down the mountain.
"We have been tricked!" screamed the
Sky People. "Rabbit has stolen the fire!"

Rabbit ran and the Sky People followed.

They made a great rain.

They made thunder
and lightning.

They made sleet.

They made snow.

But the wonderful head-dress with the
resin-coated feathers burned brightly.

Rabbit was soon tired.
"Squirrel! Take the head-dress,"
he gasped. Squirrel took
the head-dress and ran.

As she went, the heat made
her tail curl up and over her back.
And so are squirrels to this day.

Squirrel was soon tired.
"Crow! Take the head-dress,"
she chattered. Crow took the
head-dress and flew. As he
went, the smoke turned
all his feathers black.
And so are crows to this day.

Crow was soon tired.
"Racoon! Take the head-dress,"
he cawed. Racoon took the head-dress
and ran. As she went, some ash
burned rings around her tail and face.
And so are racoons to this day.

Racoon was soon tired.
"Turkey! Take the head-dress,"
she panted. Turkey took the head-dress
and ran. As he went, the fire
burned all the feathers off his head
and neck. And so are turkeys to this day.

But Turkey was not a fast runner,
and the fire began to die.

"Set my tail alight," said Deer.
For in those days deer had long tails.

Deer took the fire on her tail,
and ran so fast that she made a wind
to fan the flames. Deer cried
to the trees as she passed,
flicking her tail this way and that,

"Trees, hide the fire!"
The trees took the fire and
hid it in their wood. But the
fire had burned off most of Deer's
tail. And so are deer to this day.

The Sky People returned to their
village high in the mountains.
Wood had hidden fire and they
didn't know how to find it again.
But Rabbit, leader of all mischief,
knew. It was he who showed the
animals how to find fire again
by rubbing two sticks together.
Now the animals have fire to
warm the cold winters, and light
to brighten the dark nights.